Landis Valley Museum

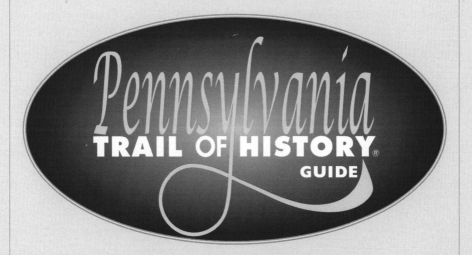

Text by Elizabeth Johnson
Photographs by Craig A. Benner

STACKPOLE BOOKS

PENNSYLVANIA HISTORICAL
AND MUSEUM COMMISSION

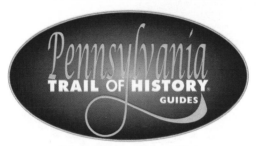

Kyle R. Weaver, Series Editor
Tracy Patterson, Designer

Published by
STACKPOLE BOOKS
5067 Ritter Road
Mechanicsburg, Pennsylvania 17055

Printed in the United States of America
2 4 6 8 10 9 7 5 3 1
FIRST EDITION

Maps by Caroline Stover

Photography
Craig A. Benner: cover, 3, 10–15, 24, 25, 28–47
Landis Valley Museum staff photographer: 5

Library of Congress Cataloging-in-Publication Data

Johnson, Elizabeth, 1947–
    Landis Valley Museum: Pennsylvania trail of history guide / text by Elizabeth Johnson ; photographs by Craig A. Benner.—1st ed.
        p. cm.—(Pennsylvania trail of history guides)
    Includes bibliographical references.
    ISBN 0-8117-2955-9
    1. Landis Valley Museum—Guidebooks. 2. Pennsylvania Dutch—History—Miscellanea. 3. Pennsylvania Dutch—Social life and customs—Miscellanea. 4. Country life—Pennsylvania—Miscellanea. 5. Pennsylvania Dutch—Pennsylvania—Landis Valley—History—Miscellanea. 6. Landis Valley (Pa.)—History—Miscellanea. 7. Landis family—Miscellanea. I. Title. II. Series.

F159.L225 J64 2002
974.8'15—dc21
                                                                          2002018905

Contents

Editor's Preface

Pennsylvania Dutch culture developed in the eighteenth century with the arrival of a multitude of German and Swiss immigrants to William Penn's province and has remained an integral part of the identity of the state. It is fitting, therefore, that this legacy is preserved in a museum complex by the Pennsylvania Historical and Museum Commission (PHMC). Stackpole Books is proud to join the PHMC in its effort to keep this heritage alive by featuring the Landis Valley Museum in this new volume of the Pennsylvania Trail of History Guides, a series of handbooks on the historic sites and museums administered by the PHMC.

The series was conceived and created by Stackpole Books with the cooperation of the PHMC's Division of Publications and Bureau of Historic Sites and Museums. Donna Williams heads the latter, and she and her staff of professionals review the text of each guidebook for historical accuracy and have made many valuable recommendations. Diane Reed, Chief of Publications, has facilitated relations between the PHMC and Stackpole from the project's inception, organized the review process with the commission, and attended to numerous details related to the venture.

For this volume, Stephen Miller, Director of Landis Valley Museum, worked closely with me in the development stages, recommended the text writer, created an effective work environment as we pored over the site's archives to find pertinent historic images, and provided many of the resources needed to make this book a reality. Craig A. Benner, who has contributed to other volumes in this series, has captured the richness and diversity of the site in his splendid photography.

Elizabeth Johnson, the author of the text, is currently Museum Educator at Fort Hunter Mansion and Park, near Harrisburg. She was formerly Museum Educator at Landis Valley Museum, where she played a pivotal role in cultivating the site's current interpretive plan. She brings that valuable experience to this guidebook, offering a concise overview of the Pennsylvania Dutch and their distinctive culture; the fascinating story of the Landis brothers and the progression of their collection of thousands of objects into a fledgling museum; and a complete tour of the complex today, including its historic buildings, numerous exhibits, and living-history demonstrations of Pennsylvania Dutch cooking, crafts, and farming practices.

Kyle R. Weaver, Editor
Stackpole Books

Introduction to the Site

At Landis Valley Museum, visitors are immersed in Pennsylvania Dutch rural life. The museum includes historic buildings and landscapes, heritage farm animals and plants, and rich and diverse collections consisting of some seventy-five thousand early farm, craft, and household objects. Visitors can experience living history programs in farm areas, watch craftspeople at work, and enjoy a wealth of authentic objects in exhibits such as the re-created late-1700s Log Farm or the original c. 1879 Landis House.

Landis Valley Museum takes its name from the crossroads where it was founded in 1925. Administered today by the Pennsylvania Historical and Museum Commission, it was created by brothers Henry Kinzer Landis and George Diller Landis, who managed it until after World War II. The section of the museum created by the Landis brothers is listed in the National Register of Historic Places. The museum today includes preserved areas of the village, as well as facilities developed over the past sixty years. In addition to over twenty exhibit areas, Landis Valley offers a full calendar of special events, workshops, and school programs; an outstanding store; and food service in its historic hotel. Its preservationist Heirloom Seed Project, with gardens, a seed catalog, and educational programs, is nationally recognized.

The Pennsylvania Dutch

S tarting in the late 1600s, chaos in Germanic Europe propelled the first wave of immigrants to Pennsylvania, attracted to the idea of greater freedom and greater prosperity for their families in the New World. William Penn, the proprietor of Pennsylvania, was an English Quaker, and like the Mennonites in Switzerland and other German-speaking areas of Europe, he was a pacifist who had suffered religious persecution. In 1677, 1682, and 1684, Penn traveled to the western Germanic regions of Rhineland-Palatinate on a mission to preach his faith. In his travels in the 1680s, he invited people to his colony, proclaiming his belief in religious freedom for all. The first Germanic group to his colony, including many recently converted Quakers, disembarked at Philadelphia in 1683.

The Protestant Reformation, which had started in the 1500s, had brought great religious upheaval to Europe. This turmoil was especially severe in the Holy Roman Empire of the German nation, where the reform began. Religious persecution had become commonplace in many regions. Often strife would ensue when a Protestant replaced a Catholic ruler of a principality, state, or region, or a leader switched religious allegiance. By 1618, the Thirty Years' War, a long series of religious struggles involving much of Europe, had begun. This war devastated the Palatinate, leaving large farming areas ruined and deserted. Estimates suggest that 70 percent of the people in the region died. The collection of independent states and principalities that then constituted the German nation declined from a population of 30 million to 20 million. In the 1680s, the Palatinate was again ravaged by the French armies of Louis XIV.

Estimates suggest that perhaps seventy-five thousand German-speaking people came to Pennsylvania between 1683 and 1820. Most left from southwestern Germany—today's Rhineland-Palatinate and Baden-Württemberg—as well as the northern cantons of Switzerland. This was a youthful emigration primarily of families; most heads of households were tradesmen and farmers. Although some desired religious

Pennsylvania Dutch Rural Life of the late nineteenth century was vividly captured by the Landis brothers in numerous photographs. This wash day scene was taken at the George Diller Farm, near New Holland, in the 1880s. LANDIS VALLEY MUSEUM

Regions of Emigration. In the eighteenth century, rampant persecution led many religious dissenters to leave their homelands in the Palatinate, Württemberg, Baden, Alsace, and Switzerland. Some of these German-speaking Europeans sought refuge in Holland before emigrating to Pennsylvania.

that faith had to be coupled with good works. The Anabaptist movement and the Mennonite sect spread rapidly throughout much of central Europe. By the 1690s, Jakob Amman, who lived in the Alsace region, led a group away from the Mennonites to establish the Amish sect. Amman and others believed that shunning was not being used sufficiently to discipline wayward members, and that Mennonites were becoming too worldly. Still observed by the Amish today, shunning is a practice that restricts church members from associating with other members who have violated certain church rules. After the Amish emigrated to America, their sect eventually died out in Europe.

Most of the early immigrants came from what are today Germany and Switzerland, but they also emigrated from German-speaking areas now in countries such as France and the Czech Republic. Although a majority of the Colonial German immigrants came to Pennsylvania, they also landed in New York, Virginia, and the Carolinas, and some migrated southward into Maryland and Virginia through the Shenandoah Valley and westward into the Midwest.

freedom, to a great extent the immigrants were seeking a more stable and prosperous life in America. Most settlers were church people, Lutherans or Reformed. Some were even seeking freedom *from* religion.

Only a small percentage of the immigrants (about 10 percent) were from the plain sects, such as the Mennonites, Amish, and Dunkards. These sects arose during the Protestant Reformation, believing in the radical tenets of separation of church and state, adult rather than infant baptism, and pacifism. Called Anabaptists, they believed in an unworldly life that eschewed materialism. By 1536, Menno Simons, formerly a Catholic priest, became an Anabaptist in the Netherlands. Unlike other Anabaptist leaders, he believed

GERMAN SETTLEMENT

Viewing American immigration from the earliest period to the present, Scott Swank, in his book *Arts of the Pennsylvania Germans*, has determined that Germanic people are the largest immigrant group and the most evenly distributed throughout the United States. The Penn-

PENNSYLVANIA DUTCH OR PENNSYLVANIA GERMAN?

Originally the Pennsylvania Dutch did not see themselves as a single group. Coming from various European regions, they spoke many dialects, wore different clothing from one another, and practiced different Protestant religions. By the early 1800s, they had been Americans for a generation or two. Although many also spoke English, they used one common German dialect—the Palatinate dialect, which had become the language of the Pennsylvania Dutch.

Dutch had been the common term describing German-speaking settlers and their descendants in Pennsylvania since the Colonial period. Derived from the German word *Deutsch*, meaning German, *Dutch* is an old English word meaning the German language and those who use it. *Pennsylvania German* is an academic term that arose in the later nineteenth century to counteract the misconception that the Pennsylvania Dutch were of Holland Dutch descent.

sylvania Germans, or Pennsylvania Dutch, are a specific subset within this large group. Most scholars define them as German-speaking European immigrants in Pennsylvania between 1683 and 1820, together with their descendants.

The majority of the earliest settlers to Lancaster County were Swiss Mennonites, who first arrived by 1711 with six families. They settled central Lancaster County, having obtained ten thousand acres between Pequea Creek and the Conestoga River. The immigrants purchased the land from Penn's government, with the approval of the Conestoga Indians living in that area. In agreement with Penn's fair treatment of Indians, the Mennonites lived peaceably with the Native Americans.

The first Landis families in Landis Valley were part of the early Swiss immigration. By 1720, the scattered settlement had grown to more than sixty-six families, with five house carpenters, a bricklayer, a blacksmith, two doctors, a miller, and many farmers. Two gristmills, a sawmill, and a boring mill were in business. Before Lancaster County was established in 1729 and the town of Lancaster the next year, some Swiss

immigrants were establishing farmsteads north of what became the town of Lancaster. In 1735, a Philadelphia man reported that the Mennonites "live 60 or 70 miles off, but come frequently to town with their wagons, laden with skins (which belong to the Indian traders) butter, flour, etc."

By 1790 about 40 percent of the Pennsylvania people were of German background. The next largest group was the English/Welsh, at 30 percent, followed by the Scots-Irish, at 15 percent. At that time, Lancaster and Berks Counties had the highest concentration of Pennsylvania Dutch—over 70 percent of

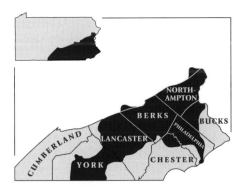

German Settlement in Pennsylvania. *By 1760, German groups had settled in heavy concentrations across Pennsylvania.*

The Fertile Lands of Southeastern Pennsylvania provided the Pennsylvania Dutch with livelihood and abundance.

their populations. The heaviest settlements of Pennsylvania Dutch have been, and remain, in the region bordered by Northampton, Bucks, and Montgomery Counties on the east; York County on the west; York and Lancaster Counties in the south; and Snyder, Union, Northumberland, and Schuylkill Counties to the north. Because of migration, concentrations of Pennsylvania Dutch can be found in western counties such as Somerset.

PENNSYLVANIA DUTCH CULTURE

The German immigrants to Penn's "Holy Experiment" settled in a temperate climate with good to remarkably fine soil for farming, adequate rain, and long growing seasons. The gently rolling Piedmont area, with its exceptionally fertile land, extends from the Philadelphia area west almost to Harrisburg, and north close to Reading. This area of earliest settlement includes some of the best farmland in America. From this area came the bounteous grain crops, the thousands of barrels of flour that made Pennsylvania the largest food-producing American colony by the 1760s. At that time, about 90 percent of the population in the colony and America were farmers. Although Pennsylvania's production of iron was the highest in the colonies, and

it exported significant quantities of lumber, its wheat sales were far more valuable.

Settlement patterns, especially in rural areas, helped create and sustain the Pennsylvania Dutch culture. Immigrant families arrived with neighbors, and sometimes entire congregations emigrated, establishing dense German enclaves. In the expansive, rural areas, distances and valleys created many isolated pockets of German settlement. The populations far from Philadelphia and other major population centers were able to maintain their Pennsylvania Dutch language well into the twentieth century. Even in the 1950s, some Dutch children growing up in mainstream-church families just forty-five minutes north of the state capital were entering school speaking only the dialect.

The Pennsylvania Dutch created homogeneous communities that maintained similar foodways, a conservative architecture, and strong ties to farming. In many areas, agriculture remained the center of life until the late 1900s. Because of the richness of the soil, the farms could be small but productive. The average-size Lancaster-area farm in the late 1700s was 135 acres, of which only about 52 acres were cleared. (By the 1950s, the typical Lancaster County farm

Log Architecture is ubiquitous in the regions where the Pennsylvania Dutch settled.

was averaging only 62 acres but was still highly productive because of intensive agricultural practices.)

Early on, Pennsylvania Dutch farmers, like most Pennsylvania farmers, were tied to a market economy. These colonists were producing not only to feed themselves, but also to sell excess grain, meat, hides, and other goods at market. Everyone on the farm worked, from young children to grandparents. Children as young as four were expected to do chores such as gathering eggs or picking dirt from wool. Depending on the need, women worked in the orchards or fields, barnyard, or house. Their usual tasks included dairying, preserving food, tending the kitchen garden and the poultry, making beer and alcoholic fruit beverages, cooking, spinning, and making simple clothing. Men raised the large animals, cleared and prepared the fields, grew the large crops, tended to the fencing, repaired the equipment, and made most of the commercial transactions. Everyone helped at butchering and harvest times.

The Pennsylvania Dutch popularized log architecture, building mostly houses and barns of logs in the countryside. Even houses in town were often of logs. They often put thatched roofs on their barns. For springhouses, the fire-prone bakehouses, and smokehouses, roofs were commonly of clay tile. Whether in town or country, some of their best houses were of stone, often limestone. After the early 1800s, there was a noticeable shift to building with brick, although some houses continued to be built of logs or stone. Today central Pennsylvania is the core area for early American log structures.

The Pennsylvania Dutch also brought from continental Europe the impressive "Pennsylvania" barn, also called a bank barn because of the bank or hillside at the rear of the barn that allowed wagons and large equipment to enter at the second floor. The feature that distinguishes this barn from all others, however, is its front forebay, or overhang, which allows for shelter below

Pennsylvania Dutch Women were responsible for food preparation, including the smoky task of boiling applebutter.

Crafts. Though the Pennsylvania Dutch were mostly farmers, they became known for their practical but decorative crafts.

farmers, thousands of craftspeople supplied their needs and the needs of those who supported the agricultural economy. They built the Conestoga wagons and the barns, fashioned the pottery tiles for roofs and plates for pie baking, and produced ironware for door hinges, kitchen utensils, and farm implements. Imported goods from Europe and around the world were readily available in towns and cities; well-to-do colonists wore clothes made from imported fabrics, drank from European glassware, and sat on English-style chairs. But many of the everyday needs, from homespun wool cloth and simple chairs to barrels, harnesses, and shoes, were increasingly made locally. And some Colonial artisans created fine furniture, silver, pewter, and buildings.

German craftsmen were heavily involved in this production. They were particularly concentrated in papermaking and printing, cabinetry and clockmaking, leather tanning, shoe and hat manufacturing, and cloth production. German workers made up the vast majority of men mining and producing iron in Colonial Pennsylvania. The Pennsylvania Dutch have long been noted for their metalworking skills as gunsmiths, blacksmiths, tinsmiths, and coppersmiths, and they cast iron stove plates so that their fellow Germans could continue to use heating stoves in America. Many of the potters were Pennsylvania Dutch, producing utilitarian wares for kitchen use, tableware, and even roofing. They are perhaps best known for their decorative, commemorative redware. This redware, which actually constituted only a minority of their

and a larger second floor above. These often massive barns still stand on the Pennsylvania Dutch landscape in large numbers. Another Germanic structure seen on Pennsylvania farms into the 1800s was the hay barrack, a simple form with an adjustable thatched roof that moved up and down on four tall posts, protecting hay stacked beneath it.

By the late 1700s, hundreds of mills were working in southeastern Pennsylvania—most to turn grain into flour, but others to transform timber into lumber and seeds into oil. To haul these goods to market towns and to Philadelphia for export, Pennsylvania Dutch in Lancaster County used the sturdy and capacious Conestoga wagon. Developed before 1750, it was the tractor-trailer of Colonial America. This was the vehicle that enabled the agricultural bounty of Pennsylvania to reach ships bound for Europe, the Caribbean, and other far ports.

Although the majority of the early generations of American colonists were wares, was embellished with sgraffito—incising through slip, a fine liquid clay trailed for writing or decorative effects—or with slip alone.

Craftspeople in Philadelphia and the bigger towns made objects that they would sell both to their English neighbors and to their fellow Germans. In the society in which they lived, the English held the political and financial power. In the town of Lancaster, about 66 percent of the population was German between 1760 and 1790, but the English population controlled the legal and political systems, as well as much of the finances. For numerous German Americans, to succeed was to assimilate. English was the language of commerce and of the courthouse, especially in Philadelphia. Over time, assimilation accelerated, especially in the larger population areas, where large numbers of English and other groups lived.

Children of German settlers were Americans. The ties of the Pennsylvania communities to Europe grew more remote as time passed, even though a flow of immigrants continued. They slowly became more adapted to "American" options not in keeping with their ethnic background. Some anglicized their names and learned English. They might keep their Germanic benches and heating stoves but build a house with an English-style center hall. Although they might continue to use a German hanging cupboard and colorfully painted chest, wealthier Germans might also purchase an English chest of drawers or even a tea table. And Pennsylvania Dutch craftsmen were sometimes the artisans building those English-style houses and furnishings. Many continued to use German techniques and designs while adopting certain English styles and forms.

By the 1840s, industrialization was beginning to change significantly the

Pennsylvania Dutch Pottery and Metalware.

culture of the Pennsylvania Dutch and American society. Professional craftspeople, such as potters and furniture makers, continued to thrive in the more rural, conservative communities. In urban areas, however, textile factories produced cheap cotton and wool. Women, therefore, ceased spinning at home, and demand for the local weavers' goods declined. Many shoemakers and blacksmiths shut up their shops, sometimes going to work in the very factories that put them out of business. The *Fraktur* artists, usually schoolmasters associated with the Pennsylvanian German Lutheran and Reformed churches, found their hand-drawn and hand-painted documents, such as birth certificates, replaced

13

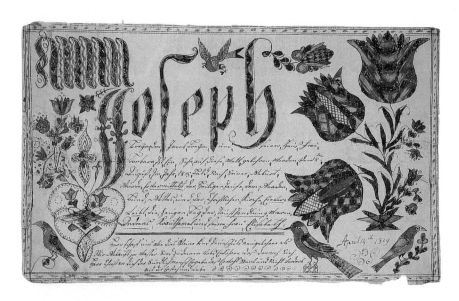

Fraktur. *Pennsylvania Dutch artists illustrated wall charts, house blessings, and birth and baptismal certificates with ornate, illuminated drawings.*

with printed documents. The end of most significant hand production of goods meant the loss of much of the cultural expression of the Pennsylvania Dutch and of other American ethnic groups as well.

Language is perhaps one of the most important cultural markers. The establishment of public schooling during the 1830s in Pennsylvania accelerated the diminished use of the Pennsylvania Dutch dialect. Both World War I and II, which stirred strong anti-German sentiment, contributed to further decreases. These factors, in addition to the mass media, the growing commercialization of America, and the continual shrinking of the farming population, have all but wiped out the general use of the dialect. Now only the plain sects, particularly the Amish, and a few of the old mainstream-church Pennsylvania Dutch in Berks, Lehigh, and Lebanon Counties, use this language daily. Because of continued Amish emphasis on separation from the world, they have maintained their dialect. Many Mennonites, on the other hand, have adopted a more modern lifestyle, and few still speak Pennsylvania Dutch.

Certain Pennsylvania Dutch cultural traditions have become part of mainstream American culture—the Easter rabbit and the Christmas tree, for example. Foodways are usually one of the last cultural expressions to remain, and the Pennsylvania Dutch still love their pretzels, pork and sauerkraut (especially on New Year's Day), chicken pot pie, red beet pickled eggs, and various bolognas and sausages. Pennsylvania Dutch quilts, which continue to be made by Amish, Mennonites, and some church Dutch, are collected and used across America. Their bold, colorful patterns put a Germanic stamp on a craft originally learned from English Pennsylvanians.

Today anyone looking for a Pennsylvania Dutch presence in central Pennsylvania need only note German names in the phone book or on road and business signs. If you are traveling in the countryside, you will drive by many Pennsylvania Dutch barns with forebays and pass many log houses sheathed with modern siding. You will pass through small, linear Pennsylvania Dutch villages with houses close together. You might notice how few nineteenth-century houses were built in the popular architectural styles, such as Greek Revival or Italianate. Until the 1900s, most Pennsylvania Dutch in villages and rural areas seemed to ignore the prevailing building trends. Today many Pennsylvania Dutch cultural artifacts, from mills to manuscripts to pottery, still exist. More important, the Pennsylvania Dutch people continue to thrive at the same time that they evolve.

Sauerkraut, a basic Pennsylvania Dutch side dish, is made from cabbage, traditionally shredded on a Grout-hovvel, *or cabbage plane, then fermented in its own juices and salt. The Pennsylvania Dutch served it with pork for dinner on New Year's Day, a custom that continues in the present culture.*

History of Landis Valley Museum

L andis Valley Museum's richly lay-
ered story is the history of an early
Pennsylvania Dutch settlement, an
unusual farm family, and the ongoing
creation and exploration of a wonder-
fully diverse collection of artifacts. When
brothers Henry Kinzer Landis (1865–
1955) and George Diller Landis (1867–
1954) opened their museum in 1925 at
their Landis Valley residence, the area
had been a small Pennsylvania Dutch
settlement since the mid-1800s. Their
ancestors gave this village and the surrounding valley its name.

These forebears were part of the first
group of Europeans—German-speaking
Mennonites—to come to the Lancaster
area. The Landis brothers were the sev-
enth generation of Landises to live in the
county. Their Mennonite ancestor Benjamin Landis brought the Landis name
there around 1749 when he married
Ann Snavely, the daughter and sole heir
of a successful Mennonite settler. Ann
had grown up on a Landis Valley farmstead with more than two hundred acres.
By 1751, Benjamin and Ann owned the
Snavely homestead. (The 1728 house
still stands about a half mile south of
the museum at 2201 Oregon Pike.)
When Benjamin died in 1787, he owned
905 acres in the area.

SETTLEMENT IN LANDIS VALLEY

The Landises and Snavelys had come
with thousands of other hopeful German immigrants to Pennsylvania in the
1700s and early 1800s. They laid claim
to some of the best agricultural land in
America. Landis Valley and the surrounding area are part of the limestone
lowlands of the Pennsylvania Piedmont–Lancaster Plain and have an
unusually favorable environment for
agriculture. With rich soil, a mild climate, and adequate rainfall allowing for
a long growing season, this region
enabled Colonial Pennsylvania to pros-
per because of its bountiful production
and export of grain and flour.

To this intensive farming, Lancaster
added the tobacco crop after the Civil
War. Very valuable but labor-intensive,
tobacco increased the prosperity of the
area, including the Landis brothers' family. Tobacco money helped pay for the
brothers' expenses at Lehigh University.
Because of this golden leaf, Lancaster
County grew more profitable farm prod-
ucts than any other U.S. county from
1880 to 1920.

The first settlers, Native Americans,
had also farmed in the Landis Valley
area. About one thousand years ago, the
Algonquians were part-time farmers as

*Landis Valley Museum. Some of the Landis brothers' earliest museum artifacts are displayed
here.* LANDIS VALLEY MUSEUM

Tobacco Farming in Landis Valley, c. 1890.
LANDIS VALLEY MUSEUM

well as hunters and gatherers. But Native American occupation of Landis Valley was only a memory by the Victorian era. As early as the mid-1700s, few lived in the valley. Indeed, disease and white settlement had removed most of them from eastern Pennsylvania. As boys, in the 1870s and 1880s, the Landis brothers had gathered their stone implements, including axes, spear points, and pestles. With their father, they searched the plowed fields of the family farm in Landis Valley for these relics. First exhibited in their boyhood attic museum, or "roost," these artifacts are still part of the museum's holdings.

The successful development of Landis Valley by the Pennsylvania Dutch was linked to good transportation. By the 1730s, an official road was running north from the community of Lancaster, past the Snavely House to a nearby mill. Called the Great Road, then the Reading Road, and today the Oregon Pike, it once ran through the heart of what is today the museum. In the 1810s, the Landis brothers' grandfather, Drover Henry, in his teens at the time, drove a Conestoga wagon down this road, as his forefathers had, to deliver Landis flour and whiskey to Philadelphia. Not until the 1840s did people drive their goods for market down the Reading Road to Lancaster for shipment on railroad cars.

To the north, closer to the area that became the village, Colonial families continued to create new farmsteads and new businesses. By 1779, the shop of shoemaker Philip Hess stood on the road within view of the present Blacksmith Shop. From the late 1700s well into the 1800s, a blacksmith worked in that location, including blacksmith-farmer Jacob Landis. Near this shop, Landis and his wife, Elizabeth, developed a small but handsome farmstead between 1805 and the 1840s, today the museum's Brick Farmstead.

By the 1820s, the present-day Landis Valley Road, which runs east-west, crossed Reading Road. Next to this intersection, Mennonites built a meetinghouse and a cemetery in the late 1840s on land donated by Drover Henry, grandfather of the Landis brothers. Today the cemetery remains a landmark, and a later brick church building stands within a block of where the original log one stood. Henry Stark's log house, wagon-making shop, and stables also stood in Landis Valley during the 1840s.

In the 1850s, Jacob Landis Jr., of the Brick Farmstead, erected the Landis Valley House Hotel on the northeast corner of Reading Road and Kissel Hill Road, about 275 yards south of the complex. This became the center of the village. Here Landis served passengers waiting for the stagecoach, men seeking an alcoholic lift from winter doldrums, or people traveling to Lancaster to shop or do business at the courthouse. Over the decades, many customers heatedly discussed sales at the livestock auction next door or wondered what the year's tobacco crop would bring. The post office in the hotel, there briefly in the 1850s and then operating from 1872 to 1913, brought in more foot traffic.

By 1870, a small village was emerging. The *Directory of Lancaster Co.,*

1869–70 lists fifty-five Landis Valley residents (mostly men) and their occupations. There were twenty-seven farmers, fourteen laborers, a gentleman, two seamstresses, two blacksmiths, an innkeeper/postmaster, and a wagon maker. Those workers on the lower end of the economic scale—the laborers and possibly the seamstresses and the blacksmiths—were probably renters or tenants. In Colonial or Victorian America, many farm workers and other laborers were hired help who owned no land or real property. The founders' wealthy grandfather, Drover Henry Landis, was listed as a farmer; the brothers and their immediate family had not yet moved back to Landis Valley.

When the brothers were boys in the mid-1870s, their family relocated to Landis Valley from a more southern part of Lancaster County, as their ailing grandparents needed care. Their father, Henry H. Landis, dutifully nursed, washed, and dressed his aging father. After Drover Henry died in 1876, the family established a new farm at the center of Landis Valley within the farmstead once run by Drover Henry. Their new farmhouse was nearly opposite the hotel.

The Landis Farm, c. 1892.
LANDIS VALLEY MUSEUM

A quick look at the *Lancaster City and County Directory, 1882–1883* tells us something about their neighbors. Stating that Landis Valley "contains 50 inhabitants" who could take the "Daily stage" to Lancaster for 25 cents, it gives a commercial listing of eleven Landis Valley people or businesses: a cigar manufacturer, a cigar packing company, two dealers in leaf tobacco, a veterinary surgeon, a carpenter, a wheelwright, a shoemaker, a blacksmith, a hotel manager, a thresher, and a lime burner. The last refers to the brothers' father, Henry H., who worked a small limestone quarry on his farm and made lime there.

THE LANDIS BROTHERS AND THE ORIGIN OF THE COLLECTION

By the 1880s, the Landis brothers, who worked on the family farm, were becoming collectors. They stockpiled a variety of objects such as books, birds' eggs, fossils, and minerals. The brothers were encouraged in their intellectual explorations by their parents and teachers; both boarded at the nearby Lititz Academy and then studied engineering at Lehigh University.

Although each man worked in the American West for a time, Henry K. spent most of his career in New York City as an editor of technical journals from 1894 to 1924. With his brother in New York, George stayed home to help run the family farmstead. For years, he was also manager of the city of Lancaster's sanitation department. Perhaps his major contribution to the museum was his collection of hunting equipment, from firearms to fishing spears. He had started to purchase pistols and rifles when he was fifteen. This collection reflected his longtime interest in hunting, especially for big game. An excellent marksman, he often traveled to the West and to Clinton County, Pennsylvania, to hunt.

NO ORDINARY FAMILY

The average person does not create a museum. The Landis Valley founders were far from the norm, and so was their upbringing. Their farm family consisted of the parents Emma Diller (1842–1929) and Henry H. Landis (1838–1926), and siblings Henry Kinzer (1865–1955), George Diller (1867–1954), and Nettie May (1879–1914), the darling of the family.

Like many Americans born in the 1860s, everyone, including children, worked on the farm. But Henry K. Landis wrote in his autobiography that "his parents were not strict, but unusually liberal." They rarely attended church and belonged to no congregation. The parents allowed their children great freedom to explore intellectually and physically. All three children attended college, which was unusual in Victorian America.

Mother Emma came from a prosperous Pennsylvania Dutch farm family. She had attended Linden Hall, a private school in nearby Lititz. In photographs she appears dour and severe, but little is known of her personality. No writings by her survive, nor any descriptions of her except in her husband's diary.

We know a great deal about father Henry H. because of his diaries spanning many years and a fragment of his 1894 autobiography.

Very interested and involved with his children, he "had little taste" for farming, according to son Henry. The father's diary reveals a man who spent all night caring for his sick baby daughter, showed his children the stars with his telescope, and let them stay home from school in bad weather. He wrote after his father's death in 1876 of his great disappointment in receiving only life use of the 120-acre family farm well situated on Reading Road. Whether he was ill suited for farming or unhappy because he felt trapped, he detailed times of excessive drinking and of great unhappiness with his wife. He speculated on wheat and at times lost thousands of dollars. Perhaps this accounts for the "1885 Sheriff's Public Sale, H. H. Landis Property" in the archives, which lists various farm animals, equipment, and even three acres of tobacco.

The youngest child, Nettie May, was the sunshine of the family, someone they all loved. Her lively, fun-loving personality is obvious from the surviving fragment of her diary. She attended a local teacher's college (now Millersville University) but did not graduate because of illness. Her health never improved. In 1914, Nettie May, then in her mid-thirties, died from tuberculosis at a sanitorium in Utah.

The Landis Family, c. 1905. From left: brothers Henry K. and George, sister Nettie, mother Emma, and father Henry H. LANDIS VALLEY MUSEUM

George was a reserved man. Like his brother, he never married and was viewed as somewhat eccentric. He loved cats and in his later years kept up to twenty of them. A Lititz Academy report card of all A's suggests his intelligence. He coauthored two articles with his brother on Lancaster rifles and their accessories. There is no other known writing by George—no interviews, no letters, no diaries. The papers of Henry K., on the other hand, are voluminous, including an autobiography, letters, journals, and articles for publication. He was very self-conscious about leaving his writings for posterity; they say a great deal about the facts of his life but little about his feelings. His papers reveal a gregarious person of enormous curiosity, physical energy, and wide-ranging interests. He was an avid photographer since the 1880s and taught the subject at a New York high school. In his New York years, Henry was also a gymnast, played in amateur orchestras, won sailing trophies, founded a local magazine, and sang in a church choir.

By 1910, the Landis brothers were beginning to collect avidly, attending many sales and buying cheap lots of objects. Most of their buying was in Lancaster County and surrounding counties. They usually bought inexpensive, ordinary objects, from millstones to pottery to plows. No doubt their purchases reflected both their interest in everyday Pennsylvania Dutch history and their middle-class pocketbooks. They stood outside the league of wealthy collectors and museum builders like Henry Du Pont or Henry Ford. One old-time collector explained that the brothers were called "nickel men," buying for 5 cents a basket filled with assorted objects. Today people view their many purchases of rye straw baskets, butter molds, and other small household objects with consider-ably more respect. The brothers also continued to build their library, which included hundreds of volumes about the Pennsylvania Dutch.

Henry, the spark plug of the partnership, had the drive and vision to create a museum. His goal was to preserve the vanishing culture of his ancestors for the education of the public. He wrote of "the necessity to do something to put on record what is quietly but surely slipping through our fingers into oblivion." He believed that since "these Dutch people have distinct characteristics and have achieved nation-wide distinction for their sterling qualities . . . it is important that attention should be called to their culture and standards, through those tools of their crafts and arts and customs that are obtainable." Henry wanted to make their past, with which he so identified, visible and accessible by displaying the great array of their artifacts. He also wrote journal articles about the objects and their original uses. In retirement, he learned the Pennsylvania Dutch dialect as part of his work to preserve his heritage. From 1931 to 1944, he wrote a weekly newspaper column in the dialect for the Lancaster *Intelligencer*.

THE DEVELOPMENT OF THE MUSEUM

Both Landis brothers retired and were living with their octogenarian parents in Landis Valley by 1924. The next year, they opened their Barn Museum. The death of their father in 1926 meant they inherited the family farm. By the late 1940s, they had sold off most of the acreage to support themselves and their museum. The first museum building was the Stable, now rebuilt. In 1939, the Landis brothers erected the Yellow Barn for a second exhibit building. Henry believed that people would better appreciate and understand an object when

The Museum in Its Early Days, c. 1940.
LANDIS VALLEY MUSEUM

viewing it with a sympathetic guide. Usually Henry was that guide. He did not write exhibit labels, install historical rooms, or provide dioramas of historical scenes. His exhibits were much like those of many contemporary historical societies and history museums, including great numbers of objects with few interpretive devices.

By the 1930s, the museum had attracted the interest of the Carl Schurz Foundation. The wealthy Reading, Pennsylvania, industrialist Gustave Oberlaender had created the foundation to foster the appreciation and study of the German culture. Seeing the brothers' collections as an opportunity to promote the Pennsylvania Dutch culture, the foundation agreed to pay for the construction of new exhibit buildings through its Oberlaender Trust. As a result of this support, the museum took a major step forward. It became incorporated as the Landis Valley Museum in 1940, with the brothers' donation of about three acres of land, the exhibit buildings, and selected portions of their collection. Henry and George Landis served as two of the nine directors of the board. They

George and Henry K. Landis, c. 1950.
LANDIS VALLEY MUSEUM

were also the curators, with a paid assistant, Dr. Felix Reichmann.

Trust money was used to build the Tavern (which housed the museum office), the Gun Exhibit Building, and two sheds for housing early vehicles and large farm implements, as well as support curatorial salaries and general operating expenses. The Landis brothers incorporated many of their collected objects, such as a hand pump, beehive ovens, and hinges and other ironwork, into the fabric of the new complex. In 1941, the museum "reopened" with a new name and vastly improved exhibit spaces. These new facilities enabled Henry to offer craft workshops, lectures, and classroom space at the museum.

Henry was a tireless promoter. His schemes for publicity poured in to the trust, from serving chicken and waffles in the Tavern to selling buttons with the museum's logo to the tourists. Landis's museum brochures show his intelligent approach to visitation: He provided a map and clear directions from Lancaster and Reading, mentioned the local bus route, and opened the museum six days

a week. Admission was free, and people were encouraged to join the Landis Valley Museum Association for $2 per year. Although World War II, with its travel restrictions, stifled visitation to Landis Valley, the visitor count grew from about fifty-five hundred in 1945 to over eleven thousand by 1947.

At that time, the trust intended to publicize Landis Valley nationally in order to highlight the Pennsylvania Dutch culture and counteract the anti-German feelings created by World War II. Money ran out, however, before their vision could be realized. During its years of support and guidance, the trust spent close to $90,000 on Landis Valley. Most of the money paid for maintenance and curatorial work. Neither the trust nor the aging Landis brothers had the museum experience or resources to further develop Landis Valley. The brothers lacked the knowledge and the discipline to catalog or interpret the collections professionally.

By the late 1940s, the trust, running low on money, was at the end of its support. The Landis brothers had been concerned about the future of their museum since the 1930s. They had no money to secure its future with an endowment or trust. Years of correspondence, discussions, and negotiations with various state officials proved fruitful, however. Henry, the museum's board of directors, and the trust came to an agreement with the Commonwealth of Pennsylvania. On January 1, 1953, the commonwealth received the land, buildings, and collections of the museum, as well as the land, buildings, and some of the private collections of the Landis brothers. In return, the brothers received life interest in the house and lifetime appointments as curators, and retained some of their collections. By this time, George was eighty-five and Henry eighty-seven.

The Pennsylvania Historical and Museum Commission (PHMC) assumed control of Landis Valley, but the ever-persevering Henry continued to offer ideas for the museum, even during 1955, the year of his death. George had died the year before. For decades, the Landis brothers had worked together to establish and operate the museum. Although they often disagreed and fought, they succeeded in a monumental work of many decades. They had preserved many thousands of historic Pennsylvania Dutch objects for the education and enjoyment of the public. The brothers' museum would survive.

THE MUSEUM IN RECENT YEARS

PHMC wanted to develop a Pennsylvania farm museum and saw the Landis Valley Museum as a vehicle for this goal. They immediately changed the museum's name to reflect the new direction: the Pennsylvania Farm Museum of Landis Valley. By the 1960s, the agency had developed extensive plans to change the museum. From that decade into the 1970s, they expanded the Farm Museum greatly with land acquisitions, new buildings, and historic structures moved from other areas of Lancaster County. Residents of Landis Valley moved out as the commonwealth purchased their property, sometimes using eminent domain. By the mid-1970s, the main public road through the museum was closed to traffic. The village of Landis Valley had been transformed from a residential area into a museum.

Now a paid staff offered workshops, festivals, tours, and living-history craft and farm demonstrations. Visitors could see a reconstructed 1700s log farm, an authentic early 1800s Landis Valley farmstead and numerous other new exhibits. These included period buildings moved to the museum, such as the Blacksmith

KEEPING
TRADITION ALIVE

Many of the color photographs in this book were taken at Landis Valley Museum during Harvest Days, an annual event that presents the lifestyles of the Pennsylvania Dutch, roughly between 1740 and 1940, through demonstrations of open-hearth cooking, farming practices, musical performances, and traditional trades and crafts. Contact the site for more information on the event and on other programs held throughout the year (see page 47).

Shop and the Schoolhouse. The commonwealth had paid for new construction, such as the Country Store and the Visitor Center, as well as the acquisition of numerous Landis Valley properties, including the Landis Valley House Hotel; the Isaac Landis House, Barn, and Feed Mill; and the land where the parking lot and the museum store are now located.

In the 1980s, PHMC reexamined the focus of the museum. Since the scope of the museum was wider than the farm theme, and the exhibits had never interpreted farming outside the central Pennsylvania area, PHMC and Farm Museum staff decided to return to the earlier name and focus of the museum.

After that decision, the museum put greater emphasis on research and the development of new educational programs about the Pennsylvania Dutch. The Landis Valley Associates, the museum's nonprofit support group, formed in 1959, aided this growth by greatly increasing resources to the museum.

The Heirloom Seed Project, begun in 1986, notably improved the authenticity of the gardens and the orchard. More important has been its preservation of Pennsylvania Dutch plant material with its seed collection, seed catalog, workshops, and special events.

In the last decade, management of

HEIRLOOM SEED PROJECT

The Heirloom Seed Project (HSP) is a preservation effort that is currently researching, testing, or preserving over two hundred varieties of vegetables, herbs, and ornamentals that had historical significance to the Pennsylvania Dutch between 1740 and 1940. In the 1990s, the project received a national award from the American Association for State and Local History for its successful work. A large group of volunteers provides most of the HSP labor.

Not only does HSP save historical plant material for future generations with a detailed cataloging and preservation system, but it also makes this material available to the public in a variety of ways. Its yearly seed catalog and reference guide enables people to purchase seeds at a reasonable cost and provides accurate descriptive and growing information about them. Workshops, including one on apple tree grafting, give people in-depth information that helps keep historical plant material extant. Held annually on Mother's Day weekend, the very popular HSP Herb and Garden Faire event is Pennsylvania's largest sale of heirloom plants. It also includes an outstanding selection of herbal wares.

A visitor to Landis Valley will see the Heirloom Seed Project's work in the highly authentic gardens in the two farmsteads. The museum store also carries the HSP catalog and some of its seeds.

the collections has greatly improved. The work culminated in the opening of the Landis Collections Gallery in 2000. This building provides ideal processing facilities and storage for tens of thousands of objects, while allowing visitors to see more of the collections. Today Landis Valley continues to upgrade the care of its collections, and there are plans for building new exhibition areas and storage facilities. Work is also going forward to interpret Lancaster farming in the twentieth century.

In 2000, the section of the museum developed by the Landis brothers was listed in the National Register of Historic Places. The museum received this designation because of the Landis brothers' successful efforts to preserve and present their ethnic heritage. In the new century, the Commonwealth of Pennsylvania, aided by the Landis Valley Associates, continues the vision of the Landis brothers—to tell the story of the Pennsylvania Dutch while preserving their history.

Visiting the Site

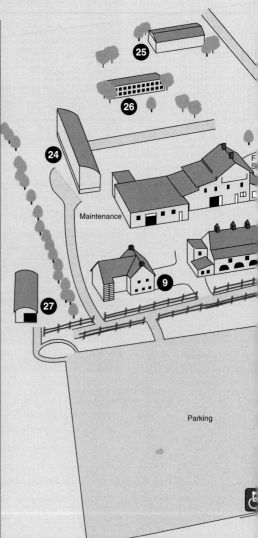

SITE LEGEND

1. Visitor Center
2. Print Shop and Leatherworking Shop
3. Log Farm
4. Brick Farmstead
4. Jacob Landis Farmhouse
4A. Grossmutter House
4B. Stone Bank Barn
5. Blacksmith Shop
6. Transportation Building
7. Landis Valley House Hotel
8. Maple Grove School
9. Steam Engine Building
10. Country Store
11. Firehouse
12. Tin Shop
13. Landis House and Stable
14. Pottery Shop
15. Yellow Barn
16. Erisman House
17. Tavern
18. Gun Shop
19. South Courtyard Shed
20. North Courtyard Shed
21. Textile Processes Building and Garden
22. Isaac Landis House, Barn, and Feed Mill
23. Weathervane Museum Store
24. Landis Collections Gallery
25. Wagon Storage Facility*
26. Chicken Coop*
27. Hands-On Museum

Restrooms

Picnic Tables

Handicapped access

Food service

* Not open to the public

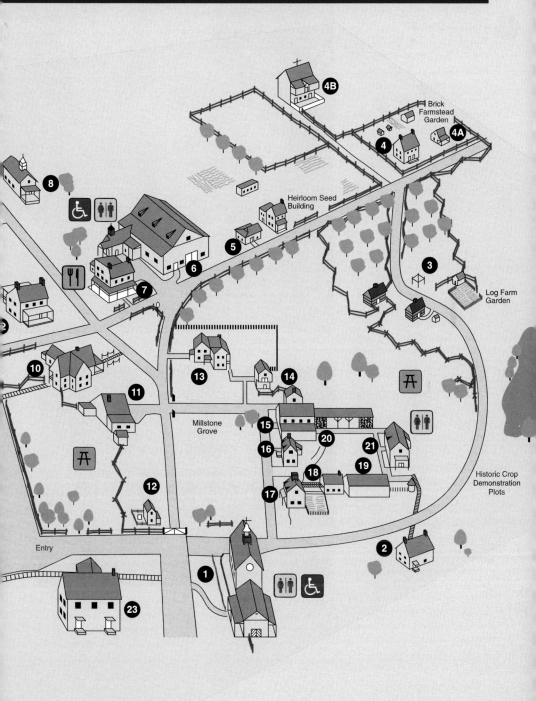

4B

Brick
Farmstead
Garden

4A

4

Heirloom Seed
Building

8

5

6

7

3

Log Farm
Garden

10

11

13

14

Millstone
Grove

15

16

20

21

19

18

17

12

Historic Crop
Demonstration
Plots

2

Entry

1

23

① VISITOR CENTER

This structure was built in 1969 to suggest an eighteenth-century market house. It contains the admissions area, the orientation video, a changing exhibit space, rental space, and offices.

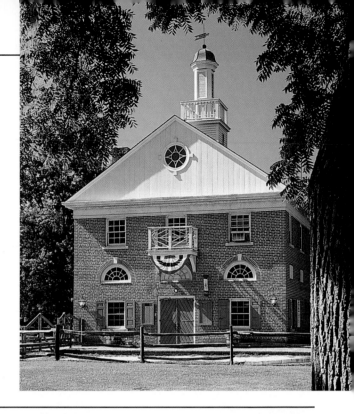

② PRINT SHOP AND LEATHERWORKING SHOP

Print Shop. A small country shop like this would have printed broadsides—posters and announcements—for rural and village people. The printer also could have produced pamphlets, a weekly paper, and even books. Printing was an expanding craft in the growing Lancaster area.

In 1810, fifteen printers worked in the town of Lancaster; by 1850, forty-five worked there. From the Colonial times through 1900, printers produced at least 275 newspapers in Lancaster County.

The exhibit represents a shop from the first half of the nineteenth century. Dominating the workspace is a c. 1826 Ramage press, invented by Scotsman Adam Ramage. It is one of only six such presses that have survived from the more than 1,250 presses he made. Ramage was building presses in Philadelphia by 1799. His cheap and lightweight presses were shipped as far as South America and the West Coast. When the Landis Valley press was built, news traveled only as fast as a ship or a horse could move. The printer was of major importance in the distribution of news and knowledge. The telegraph, telephone, radio, television, and Internet were not yet rivals to the print media.

Originally owned by the nearby Landis Valley Mennon-

ite Church, the building was acquired and moved a short distance to become a museum building. The rear corner closest to the Visitor Center is covered with Plexiglas, making its log structure visible. Although three exterior walls of the building are solid log, the front wall is timber framed, perhaps to allow more easily for two front entrances. Early Mennonite meetinghouses typically had separate front entrances for men and women.

Leatherworking Shop. This exhibit features leatherworking equipment from the 1800s and a variety of leather goods made in that period. Many early Americans plowed with a horse, rode horseback, or drove a horse and wagon and therefore needed the services of a saddler. Except for shoes and boots, which were made by the shoemaker, the saddler created all the goods of heavy leather, from saddles and harnesses to trunks. If the saddler worked in the countryside, as

springtime approached he would stop at customers' farms to ready their harnesses for field work.

Lancaster—both town and county—was a leatherworking center. In 1760, about 25 percent of the craftspeople were leatherworkers, including thirty-four shoemakers and nineteen saddlers in the town of Lancaster. Around 1820, the town's population of 6,600 included 48 saddlers, 121 shoemakers, and 22 tanners and curriers.

③ LOG FARM

The Log Farm was built in 1969–70 to represent a late-eighteenth-century Pennsylvania Dutch farmstead. A farmstead like this could have supported a family of eight or more. The average family owned about 135 acres, about 50 of which they would have cleared, and might have kept two or three horses, several head of cattle, five sheep, and some pigs and chickens. At this time, everyone was a worker, and the farm was a place of production of not only grain and beef, but also goods such as wool yarn and soap.

As was common in Lancaster County, the farm's two primary buildings—house and barn—are of logs. German-speaking immigrants popularized this construction in America. Because of its high percentage of German settlers, this area has one of the highest numbers of log structures in the country. Most eighteenth-century farms in the region had only one farm building, the barn. About one third of the farms had an additional outbuilding, such as a springhouse. For interest, the museum exhibits a range of outbuildings usually found only on the largest farms.

The log barn sheltered some of the large animals in harsh weather and stored grains and farm equipment. The hay barrack, with its adjustable roof, protected the hay. Nearby is the stone springhouse, with its red tile roof, where the family cooled milk, cheese, and other foods. Women used the bakehouse to make fruit pies and

30

bread—more than ten loaves at a time. People preserved meats such as hams in the smokehouse.

A Pennsylvania Dutch farm wife, like most Colonial women, had a raised-bed kitchen garden. This form was common in many European countries and produced large yields. The women typically planted fruits, vegetables, herbs, and flowers. The museum's Heirloom Seed Project maintains this garden and the one at the Brick Farmstead. The plants are authentic varieties once used on early Pennsylvania Dutch farms. Families also planted, tended, and harvested their orchards. The Pennsylvania Dutch favored apple trees and also grew cherry and peach trees. Visitors walk through an orchard of heirloom trees when traveling between the Log Farm and the Brick Farmstead.

Inside the log house is evidence of the family's ethnicity. Many Pennsylvania Dutch used an iron stove for warmth and relied on benches for seating. When the family entertained or ate in the stove room, the bold walnut *Shrank* would have been visible. This handsome piece of furniture stored clothes and bedding while signaling the family's prosperity. The parents and baby slept in the stove room, while the older children bedded down upstairs in the unheated loft. In that space were also stored dried fruit, smoked meat, and household equipment. The kitchen was a production area for cooking, making beer and alcoholic fruit drinks, producing herbal medicines, and preserving food.

4 BRICK FARMSTEAD

In 1805, a young married couple, Elizabeth and Jacob Landis, moved onto the six-acre tract that became the Brick Farmstead. At that time, the house was a small, stone, one-and-a-half-story building previously owned by a blacksmith, whose blacksmith shop also stood on the property. Here "Schmidt" Jacob, blacksmith and farmer, and his well-born wife, Elizabeth, raised their family. They were Pennsylvania Dutch and Mennonites.

The couple added on to the main house in c. 1812 and again in 1828–29, creating a substantially finer and larger brick house. In making the changes, they created two front doors. This Pennsylvania Dutch architectural feature had appeared by the early 1800s and can be seen on several Landis Valley buildings. The two doors allowed people to enter the formal room (the parlor on the left) or the informal room without intruding on any other space. This plan eliminated the need

for a hall and maintained a certain decorum and privacy.

Close to the time of their second son's marriage in c. 1840, the parents built the little house next door, now called the Grossmutter House. Jacob Jr. and his bride moved into the main house, and the aging parents moved into the small house. They were typical of many early Pennsylvania Dutch, who expanded housing on their farmstead to accommodate a new generation.

The main house represents

the 1830s occupancy of the family. Elizabeth and Jacob were in their fifties, daughter Nancy in her twenties. Jacob Jr. was a bachelor in his late teens to late twenties. Oldest son and edge tool maker "Devil John," who was in his midtwenties to midthirties, may not have been living at home. The little house reflects the widowed years of Elizabeth after 1848.

Although the museum owns no furnishings of the family, the 1848 inventory, taken at

the death of Jacob Sr., reveals much about their life. They could afford a tall clock, as well as a secretary (desk) for Jacob. More textiles, such as carpets and a cushion, were used than in the earlier era of the Log Farm. They had a stove for heating but did not own a cookstove. Though many Americans were using cookstoves by the 1840s, the Landises were older Mennonites and thus less likely to "go modern."

The family attended the Landis Valley Mennonite Church. They owned a *Martyr's Mirror*, a book about Christian martyrs in the Mennonite tradition. Jacob Sr. was a founder and builder of that church, as well as the first to be buried in its cemetery. The Mennonites and Amish are related plain sects and are pacifist. Although these sects have helped make

Lancaster famous, they have always represented only a small percentage of Pennsylvania Dutch.

This small farmstead also includes a bake oven, a raised-bed kitchen garden, and a Pennsylvania bank barn. The bank barn was built in the 1960s to represent a typical Pennsylvania Dutch barn with its useful forebay, or overhang. The ground floor usually housed horses and cattle. The upper floor stored

hay and grains, equipment, and the wagon. The original 1814 barn associated with the Brick Farmstead was dismantled in the 1930s. It stood a bit back from the road, next to and north of the little house. In front of it was a hay barrack.

The museum has an active farm program. At the barn, visitors can see historical breeds of draft horses, cattle, and poultry.

5 BLACKSMITH SHOP

Originally located just outside Gettysburg, this shop was owned by John W. Epley from 1904 until his death in the late 1950s. The earliest section was built about 1870. The forge and most of the tools date from the late 1800s to the early 1900s. As the master farrier, Mr. Epley shod the horses for Hanover Shoe Farms, renowned breeders of trotters and pacers.

In the Colonial period, the blacksmith was one of the most necessary community craftsmen. He made and repaired tools, hardware, and farm, cooking, and other household equipment, hammering heated iron into shape.

By the 1830s, factory-made ironware, including some from England, was putting independent blacksmiths out of work. Blacksmiths were increasingly found in factories rather than running their own smithies. By the late 1800s, most American blacksmiths were only repairing ironware or shoeing horses.

A Landis Valley blacksmith shop stood near here from the 1790s into the late 1800s. At least ten blacksmiths, including those who lived in the Brick Farmstead site, worked in Landis Valley between the early 1790s and 1896. Most of them were Pennsylvania Dutch.

6 TRANSPORTATION BUILDING

This structure was reconfigured about 1972 to replicate the Victorian-period livestock auction barn that once stood here. It was built over—and includes—the structure that housed an early Landis Valley commercial garage. In it are displayed horse-drawn vehicles, firefighting equipment used locally, vehicles for children, and business and trade signs.

Most of the vehicles are horse-drawn and from the 1850s to early 1900s. Horses pulled the heavy wagons, the elegant hearse, the sleighs, the fireman's hose reel, and the buggy. In early America, most people traveled by walking or by horse. Travelers moved slowly overland in the Colonial period and well into the nineteenth century. Roads were primitive, often rocky paths, sometimes filled with mud holes. By 1795, people were paying to use the first major stone-paved road in America, the Philadelphia–Lancaster Turnpike. Good roads became commonplace only after the advent of the automobile.

The Conestoga wagon was the tractor-trailer of its day. Men hitched six horses to the wagon to haul goods such as flour, whiskey, and iron to Philadelphia and elsewhere. These heavy vehicles evolved in Lancaster County. The canals and the railroads, which first carried passengers in the area during the 1830s, led to their demise.

The nineteenth- and early-

twentieth-century signs on exhibit reflect the preautomobile era. Because of the slow pace of travel, advertising signs could be smaller and less colorful than today's.

7 LANDIS VALLEY HOUSE HOTEL

A surviving building from the valley's Victorian era, the Landis Valley House Hotel was constructed in 1855–56 for Jacob Landis Jr., who grew up in Landis Valley. Such nineteenth-century establishments were common landmarks in the region. They still exist in many smaller central Pennsylvania towns as restaurants or taverns. This country hotel anchored Landis Valley as a young crossroads settlement and led to its development.

Local residents and travelers ate meals here. They drank beer and hard liquors such as whiskey in the barroom. Although a Mennonite, Jacob Landis Jr. sold alcoholic beverages at the Hotel. Mennonites in the area had not yet embraced temperance as a belief. Henry H. Landis, who lived across the street, mentioned going to the Hotel in many of his late-1800s diaries. For him and other local people, the Hotel was a social center. No doubt patrons talked long and hard about many an auction sale next door.

After food, drink, and company, travelers wanting a room had to navigate the steep, narrow stairs to the second floor. The Hotel's Victorian era is suggested by dark interior spaces, the many prints, and kerosene lights. None of the furnishings are original, including the imposing Victorian-period bar. Note the two front doors, also a feature of the Brick Farmstead main house, the Landis House, and the Isaac Landis House.

Locals picked up their mail at the Hotel between 1872 and 1913, when the Landis Valley Post Office operated here. For years, the stage picked up mail and passengers on a regular schedule at the Landis Valley House Hotel.

In 1860, Jacob Landis Jr. sold the hotel to Isaac Landis.

Jacob Jr. died in 1862. The hotel ceased to take lodgers around 1930. It continued as a popular local bar and restaurant, however, until the Commonwealth of Pennsylvania acquired it for the museum in 1967.

8 MAPLE GROVE SCHOOL

Children attended school in this building between 1890, when it was constructed, and the 1960s. In 1970, the museum moved the structure from Leola, in eastern Lancaster County, to its current site. After the state established public education in 1834, thousands of one-room schools like this one were built across rural Pennsylvania, providing schooling for first through eighth grades. At the time, most people considered an eighth-grade education to be an achievement. The law was opposed in many areas, including Manheim Township, where the museum is now located. Many people thought public education unnecessary and expensive; Manheim Township, on the other hand, already maintained four community-sponsored schools.

The blackboards are original to the building. The desks are from the period, as are the prints, clock, stove, teacher's desk, and other equipment. Children hung up their coats and jackets and stored their lunches in the entrance hall. The stove not only warmed children, but also heated up their lunches. To save money, children usually wrote on slates rather than paper.

Outside the schoolhouse are separate outhouses for boys and girls. Most rural schoolhouses had no water sources, and students carried buckets to nearby farms to fetch water. In this school, the students all drank from one cup until 1914.

In 1860, Pennsylvania had 6 high schools; by 1890, there were 180, mostly in cities and boroughs. Although reformers campaigned to make schooling more stimulating and creative, many teachers still emphasized memorization and rote work. Corporal punishment was commonplace. Teachers might hit a child with a ruler, but they also might punish students by keeping them in from recess or having them hold books with arms outstretched for a time.

In 1890s Lancaster County rural schools, a student had an even chance of having a male or a female teacher. Generally, urban schooling was better funded, because cities had wealth based on factories, offices, and transportation networks. Cities usually paid teachers better and had more modern facilities and equipment. In Lancaster County, schools in the city of Lancaster had a ten-month year in 1890, while the country and village schools averaged seven months.

9 STEAM ENGINE BUILDING

Steam power was used for farm work from the mid-1800s through the 1940s. The two early-1900s steam traction engines on display moved from farm to farm during Lancaster's harvest season. They operated the 1899 mammoth thresher also exhibited. (Threshing removes the seed of the grain from the straw after the grain has been harvested.) The engines also powered farm machinery such as balers, saws, and tobacco bed steamers.

The steam engine was an impressive sight in the field and for several decades played a major role in America's farm work. More significant, however, was the vast improvement in farm production between 1800 and 1900 because of horse-drawn farm equipment such as reapers and cultivators.

Also exhibited are a c. 1918 Frick tractor, which operated on kerosene and was used for plowing and harrowing (breaking up clods of soil), as well as running a thresher and baler by an attached belt; and a c. 1910 battery-powered electric ice wagon, which held thirty-six ice blocks and made deliveries until 1950.

10 COUNTRY STORE

The country store was once an important social and economic anchor in rural America. Today an empty or recycled store building still stands at many a crossroad settlement. This building was constructed in the early 1970s to represent a typical late-1800s country store. It includes both the store exhibit and museum administrative offices. Many of the objects on exhibit were purchased by the Landis brothers from inventories of stores that closed over seventy years ago. Museum records suggest that the sixty-one feet of shelving and a fifteen-foot counter were from the c. 1885 Sieber Store in Mifflintown, Pennsylvania. Some of the other counters came from Quentin, in nearby Lebanon County.

In such a store, people shopped and lingered to socialize. The storekeeper usually extended credit and took in customers' eggs and butter, which helped balance their accounts. Some of the goods were seasonal, such as seeds or school supplies. Most of the items were factory-made by the late 1800s. Similar to today's department store, the country store had sections such as medicines (for man and beast), crockery, tinware, fabric, glassware, seeds, tobacco, food, coffee, and tea. The post office in the rear of the store typically gave the storekeeper much daily

traffic. The example displayed dates from c. 1891.

By the late 1800s, many customers had a variety of sources for obtaining goods, especially if they lived near a city. Peddlers and wagons might deliver a wide range of goods, such as fabric, books, ice, and kerosene. A family could order items from a catalog like Sears and Roebuck's. Specialty shops and department stores in the nearby city of Lancaster lined many blocks.

11 FIREHOUSE

Built as a replica of an early rural firehouse, this building is now closed, except for special activities and rentals. The firefighting equipment is displayed in the Transportation Building.

12 TIN SHOP

The Landis Valley Tin Shop is housed in a structure built in the 1970s to resemble a toll-house. It displays a variety of tinsmithing tools and tinware from the nineteenth and early twentieth centuries. Tinware was fashioned from tinplate, iron or steel sheets coated with tin. Great Britain, where tin was mined, exported tin-plate to America. Britain claimed an almost complete monopoly on tinplate in the eighteenth and nineteenth centuries.

Starting in the 1730s, Connecticut was an early center for making tinware. By the early 1800s, tinware was growing in American popularity, and by the mid-1800s, people might own tin coffeepots, cookie cutters, lamps, or candle boxes. Tin roofing was also becoming commonplace. Some rural tinsmiths made their wares in the winter and peddled them in good weather; tinsmiths rarely farmed. Most customers purchased their tinware from a tin shop or peddler. It was sometimes given as the tenth wedding anniversary gift.

New tools and machinery allowed tinsmiths to increase their production. Pennsylvania had several tinsmiths in the eighteenth century, but their numbers began to swell in the 1810s. The city of Lancaster had seventeen tinsmiths in 1819 and twenty-nine by 1850. By the late 1800s, however, factory-made tinware, plated silver, and other machine-made wares put most independent tinsmiths

out of business. Today, sheet-metal workers use tinsmith tools to install roofing, spout-ing, and air conditioners, but they rarely work with tinplate.

39

⑬ LANDIS HOUSE AND STABLE

The Landis Brothers' House is perhaps the heart of Landis Valley Museum. Here the founders of the museum, Henry Kinzer Landis and George Diller Landis, lived. They moved into the new farmstead about 1879, as teenage boys. At Landis Valley, the Landis brothers began their collections as boys, stored their burgeoning holdings in their adult years, and operated their museum from the 1920s until their retirement in the 1950s.

Along with the family members, hired hands worked on the farm and in the house. They raised poultry, pigs, and cattle; made butter; and tended fields of wheat, oats, and the very rewarding tobacco. The children all helped with the animals and other farm work.

The prosperous-looking farmhouse was commodious, especially after the c. 1890 rear addition, which includes the current kitchen and rear porch. The parents chose to build a house typical of the time, with its playful brackets, porches, and numerous windows. As in the Brick Farmstead, the house has two front doors.

The interior of the house suggests the early 1900s, when the children were grown and son Henry was in New York. A major feature is the boldly grained (painted) woodwork in most of the rooms. Victorians liked grained woodwork and furniture because it created a livelier

pattern or more elegant-looking wood. In considerable contrast to the earlier houses in the museum, this house has machine-made furniture in the parlor, as well as wallpaper and liberal use of carpeting. The Landises, like most middle-class Victorians, had easy access to a vast array of factory-made furnishings, including rugs, lamps, and fabrics. Often relatively inexpensive, these goods allowed many Americans to have "decorated" homes for the first time.

Most of the furnishings displayed were made between 1860 and 1910 and are not documented family objects. Family pieces include the sideboard in the kitchen, the toy cradle in the study-office, and the sewing machine, cupboard, painted settee, and china in the sitting room. In the early 1900s, Emma and Nettie May decorated the china, a popular pastime for women of some means and leisure.

The c. 1880s Stable, unlike most of the Landis farmstead buildings, still stands. It has been partially reconstructed. It was the first museum exhibit building and from 1925 to 1939 was the only one.

14 POTTERY SHOP

Pottery was an important kitchenware and tableware in early America. Whether in Vermont or Georgia, people used inkwells, plates, and other inexpensive pottery. Most Pennsylvania potters or their families came from German-speaking lands. Often the potters also farmed. Colonists most commonly used a heavy pottery, called earthenware or redware, made from local clay. Potters usually lived near a clay deposit and often dug the clay themselves. Most of the redware potter's market was local.

Using a kick wheel or a mold, potters made a range of everyday redware objects. The wheel has long been the most important production tool, but potters were using molds by the late eighteenth century to produce dishes. They fashioned flowerpots, pitchers, jars, lamps, butter churns, and early on, even roof tiles. They made redware watertight by using lead glaze. This glaze could be toxic, especially if acidic food or drink was stored in the vessel.

Most redware was plain and red-brown, but potters also made decorated pottery. Sometimes they applied touches of color with oxides such as copper to make green or iron to make black. They also trailed creamy slip—fine, light clay mixed with water—to create words or strong patterns. With a few exceptions, only the Pennsylvania Dutch practiced the incising technique called sgraffito in America. In this technique, potters cut through a layer of slip to reveal a contrasting layer below. Often they used sgraffito on large commemorative plates.

The other common pottery was stoneware, particularly popular for crocks, jars, water coolers, and other storage vessels. It was safer and more durable than redware because it was harder pottery that used no lead glazing. Most stoneware was gray or buff, sometimes with cobalt blue decorations or a dark brown Albany slip. Potters decorated freehand and with stencils.

Sometimes they stamped the company name, location, and/or pot size on the vessel before firing.

Most of the American stoneware was made in the 1800s. The clay to make stoneware was found largely in New York and New Jersey deposits. Better transportation in the 1800s enabled potters to buy the clay and ship their wares at reasonable rates. Stoneware potters in Pennsylvania often located near a canal or railroad for faster, cheaper shipping.

15 YELLOW BARN

Built in 1939 with timber framing from the earlier 1814 Brick Farmstead barn, this is the first building the brothers erected for their museum exhibits. Now it is used for educational programs and rentals.

16 ERISMAN HOUSE

This solid log structure was moved from West Orange Street in Lancaster to the museum in 1962. Its construction date is unknown, but it was probably built before 1840. Clapboards cover the front, and board and batten siding sheathes the rest of the building. The log building is named after its last owner, George Erisman, who operated a doll repair shop in it.

The house is furnished to represent the early-nineteenth-century shop of a successful seamstress. Such a craftsperson typically made and repaired clothing, especially men's shirts, for local customers. Often a woman with no other means of support would become a seamstress, working out of her home.

Visitors can see a small kitchen and a workroom. Clothing and textiles, as well as sewing implements, are displayed in the second room.

Although people consider this a small house by today's American standards, the Erisman House would have been a moderate-size house in c.1800 Lancaster and early America.

---

17 TAVERN

The Landis brothers had this structure built in 1940. They used it as a display area, an office, and a library for their large book collection. The Tavern, along with the Gun Shop and two nearby stone sheds, were some of the first museum buildings. Furnished as an early-nineteenth-century tavern, this building is the size of many of the early country taverns. Some city taverns were fine and commodious, with a reading room, silverware, and private bedchambers. Most taverns, however, were small and simple, especially in the countryside. Some were filthy; many cheap taverns had bedbugs, and bedding went unlaundered for months.

Like the later country hotels, the taverns served both locals and travelers. Most of the customers were men; women were usually seen only when a sleighing party or other event was held at the tavern. Local customers stopped by for a drink, food, news, entertainment, and companionship. Work could be dull and tedious, and men escaped isolation and boredom in the tavern.

The taproom is based upon one shown in an 1813 painting

by John Krimmel (1789–1821), a German immigrant who was a genre painter in Philadelphia. The bar presides over the room. Simple furnishings include Windsor chairs, plain tables, mugs, glassware, and pewter. The birdcage and snake walking stick suggest the tastes of the tavern keeper.

The eating area and kitchen display both cooking equipment and tableware. The customers ate whatever was served; taverns offered no menus and little choice. In this room, a portrait painter might have set up for business, charging $1 per painting. A politician might have held a barbecue here to sway voters. Some people lounged and read the paper.

Tavern lodgers could have slept upstairs; drovers and wagon drivers would have slept outside. Tavern keepers who provided feed for horses charged extra for such service. For a time, the grandfather of the museum founders ran a tavern at his farm near Columbia, Pennsylvania. In the

1840s, he charged 37 ½ cents for a night's lodging, supper, and breakfast, and 25 cents to feed a horse night and morning.

18 GUN SHOP

The Landis brothers had this stone structure built in 1940 to showcase George Landis's collection of firearms and hunting equipment. Although the building is not an authentic re-creation of a gunsmith shop, many such structures were of stone or brick for safety. As well as Pennsylvania flintlock and percussion rifles, visitors will see pistols, powder horns and flasks, gunsmithing tools, animal traps, and other hunting and fishing gear. Two rifling benches and a boring machine are displayed. The famous Kentucky rifle, or Long Rifle, developed in Lancaster County, is featured in the exhibit.

By the 1760s, Pennsylvania Dutch gunsmiths had developed the elegant and accurate Long Rifle. It evolved from the German Jaeger hunting rifle and English fowling pieces (shotguns). They produced a rifle that was accurate at well over two hundred yards in the hands of a skilled marksman. It was longer, lighter, and smaller-bored than the Jaeger, the rifle German immigrant gunsmiths had known. European craftsmen had been rifling gun barrels to increase shooting accuracy for more than two hundred years. It was not, therefore, the rifling that set the Long Rifle apart, but the combination of its better balance, ease of handling, and accuracy. A gunsmith might have taken seven hundred to eight hundred hours to create an ornate Long Rifle.

Gunsmiths were some of the most skilled craftspeople in America. Those making the finer rifles had considerable abilities in ironwork, including rifling and lock making, and in woodworking, which also involved engraving skills. They often had knowledge of brass casting and metal engraving. A number of gunsmiths, however, purchased their locks (often imported) and barrels. A gunlock maker is listed as having operated in the town of Lancaster by 1759, and gun barrel makers were operating in Lancaster County by the early 1800s. Over 175 gunsmiths worked in the county between the frontier era and 1820.

19 SOUTH COURTYARD SHED
20 NORTH COURTYARD SHED

These structures were built in the 1940s to display vehicles and larger farm equipment at the same time that the Tavern and the Gun Shop were constructed. They are now program spaces.

21 TEXTILE PROCESSES BUILDING AND GARDEN

In this building, visitors will see demonstrations of some of the methods the Pennsylvania Dutch and many of their fellow Americans once used to create textiles for bedding and clothing.

Most Americans were still farming in the early 1800s. The majority owned homespun clothes for everyday wear and helped in some stages of their making. Farm families in the Northeast tended a flax patch for their linen cloth and raised several sheep for wool. The more prosperous of these people, whether they were in Pennsylvania or Vermont, owned "best clothing" made of imported fabric. The appetite for finer textiles was such that England shipped them in great quantities and varieties to Americans. Most wealthy people purchased imported fabrics and did not wear "homespun."

Visitors to this exhibit building see some of the steps once taken to create homespun linen. Demonstrators explain the raising and pro-

cessing of flax to become linen. Families sowed their flax seed thickly over an acre or two so that the plants would be crowded and grow straight. People pulled the plants to harvest them, thus saving the maximum length of fibers. They removed the seedpods for the next year's planting and sometimes to save for milling into linseed oil. The flax was retted or rotted by spreading the stalks on the grass for some weeks. This was the first step in separating the stringlike fibers from the rest of the stalk.

The exhibit includes such equipment as a break, scutch-ing knife and board, and hetchels, once used by farm families in the hard, dirty process of turning the flax plant into smooth, golden hanks of flax ready for spin-ning. Women then spun the processed flax into linen yarn on a flax wheel, a spinning wheel operated with a treadle. To count how much yarn was spun, they used a winder. Then it was off to a profes-sional weaver with the yarn. In the Pennsylvania Dutch region, most weavers were men. At home, however, women did weave linen tape on their tape looms for cap and apron strings, holding up stockings, and the like. Most families' sheets, towels, and shirts, as well as summer pants, stockings, and petti-coats (skirts), were of linen. English and New England tex-tile factories, producing cheap cotton, largely ended the pro-duction of homespun linen by the 1840s.

From the Colonial period into the early 1800s, farms in New England and the Mid-Atlantic area usually raised several sheep. In the spring, men sheared off the sheep's wool. Each fleece was separated into the sections of longer or shorter wool fibers. Old or young family members "picked" the wool to remove twigs, burrs, and clumps of dirt. Then they carded the wool into units called rolls. Carding readied the wool for spinning by straightening and aligning the fibers.

Most spinning was domestic work carried out by females in the family. They stood near the great, or walking, wheel, walk-ing many miles back and forth to spin yarn for winter clothes and bedding—coverlets, pants, scarves, skirts, and so on. Because wool yarn was used at home to knit hats, socks, and other winter clothes, women continued to spin wool yarn longer than they did linen thread. As with the linen, professional male weavers created most of the wool cloth made in the Penn-sylvania Dutch areas. Both an early walking wheel and a massive, early post and beam loom are part of the Textile Processes exhibit.

 ISAAC LANDIS HOUSE, BARN, AND FEED MILL

The *1875 Historical Atlas of Lancaster County* shows a view of this property when it was a small, new farmstead worked by the family of Isaac and Harriet Landis. The 1870s house and the arbor still stand, but the barn was replaced in c. 1900 after the original burned.

The next owner of the prop-erty, in 1927, Henry Herr Lan-

dis, operated a dairy with a milk delivery route and a feed mill. The dairy existed from 1927 to 1936. At the same time, the barn housed a feed mill powered by a diesel and then an electric engine.

Complementing these operations were the farm store and the feed mill office, located across from the barn at the wooden east end of the long, disjointed building now called Maintenance. Henry Herr Landis also ran a Case farm equipment dealership in the midsection of the building. On the far left of the building is a brick garage constructed to service the feed mill equipment during the 1940s to the 1960s.

One of several 1930s Landis poultry houses behind Maintenance survives; like many Lancaster farmers of this era, Landis was involved with poultry production on a much larger scale than previously.

 23 WEATHERVANE MUSEUM STORE

Supporting the mission of the museum, this store sells many books and handmade wares that relate to the Pennsylvania Dutch culture. Visitors will see displays of redware, *Fraktur*, paper cuttings, and other objects typical of those once produced and enjoyed by this major ethnic group. Many of the handmade wares created by museum demonstrators are sold in the store.

24 LANDIS COLLECTIONS GALLERY

This state-of-the-art facility was completed in 1998. It provides environmentally controlled storage for forty thousand objects, such as textiles, firearms, furniture, baskets, pottery, musical instruments, and paintings. Visitors can see examples from the collection in the open storage area with 110 feet of large viewing windows. Objects displayed range from a bold Pennsylvania Dutch *Shrank* to a massive Conestoga wagon. There is also a changing exhibit area.

For more information on hours, tours, programs, and activities at Landis Valley Museum, visit **www.landisvalleymuseum.org** or call **717-569-0401**.

Further Reading

Fegley, H. Winslow. *Farming, Always Farming: A Photographic Essay of Rural Pennsylvania Land and Life*. Birdsboro, Pa.: Pennsylvania German Society, 1987.

Fogelman, Aaron Spencer. *Hopeful Journeys: German Immigration, Settlement, and Political Culture in Colonial America, 1717–1775*. Philadelphia: University of Pennsylvania Press, 1996.

Friesen, Steve. *A Modest Mennonite Home*. Intercourse, Pa.: Good Books, 1990.

Garvan, Beatrice B. *The Pennsylvania German Collection*. Philadelphia: Philadelphia Museum of Art, 1982.

Gehret, Ellen. *Rural Pennsylvania Clothing*. York, Pa.: Liberty Cap Books, 1976.

Good, Merle, and Phyllis Good. *20 Most Asked Questions about the Amish and Mennonites*. Rev. ed. Intercourse, Pa.: Good Books, 1995.

Herr, Patricia T. *Amish Arts of Lancaster County*. Atglen, Pa.: Schiffer Publishing, 1998.

Hess, Clarke. *Mennonite Arts*. Atglen, Pa.: Schiffer Publishing, 2002.

The Homespun Textile Tradition of the Pennsylvania Germans: An Exhibit of the Work of Spinners, Weavers and Dyers at the Pennsylvania Farm Museum of Landis Valley. Harrisburg, Pa.: Pennsylvania Historical and Museum Commission, 1976.

Landis, Henry K. *Canoeing on the Juniata, 1888*. Harrisburg, Pa.: Pennsylvania Historical and Museum Commission and Landis Valley Associates, 1993.

The Landis Valley Cookbook: Pennsylvania German Foods & Traditions. Harrisburg, Pa.: Pennsylvania Historical and Museum Commission and Landis Valley Associates, 1999.

Lasansky, Jeannette. *To Draw, Upset, & Weld: The Work of the Pennsylvania Rural Blacksmith, 1742–1935*. University Park, Pa.: Pennsylvania State University Press, 1979.

Long, Amos. *The Pennsylvania German Family Farm*. Brunigsville, Pa.: Pennsylvania German Society, 1972.

Shoemaker, Alfred L. *Christmas in Pennsylvania*. 40th anniversary ed. Mechanicsburg, Pa.: Stackpole Books, 1999.

———. *Eastertide in Pennsylvania*. 40th anniversary ed. Mechanicsburg, Pa.: Stackpole Books, 2000.

Siegrist, Joanne Hess. *Mennonite Women of Lancaster County*. Intercourse, Pa.: Good Books, 1996.

Swank, Scott T., et al. *Arts of the Pennsylvania Germans*. New York: W. W. Norton & Co., 1983.

Weaver, William Woys. *Pennsylvania Dutch Country Cooking*. New York: Abbeville Press, 1993.

———. *Sauerkraut Yankees: Pennsylvania Dutch Foods & Foodways*. 2nd ed. Mechanicsburg, Pa.: Stackpole Books, 2002.

Yoder, Don. *Discovering American Folklife: Essays on Folk Culture and the Pennsylvania Dutch*. Mechanicsburg, Pa.: Stackpole Books, 2001.